I0818806

ASK THE UNIVERSE

ASK THE UNIVERSE

GUIDANCE, WISDOM, AND ANSWERS FROM THE COSMOS

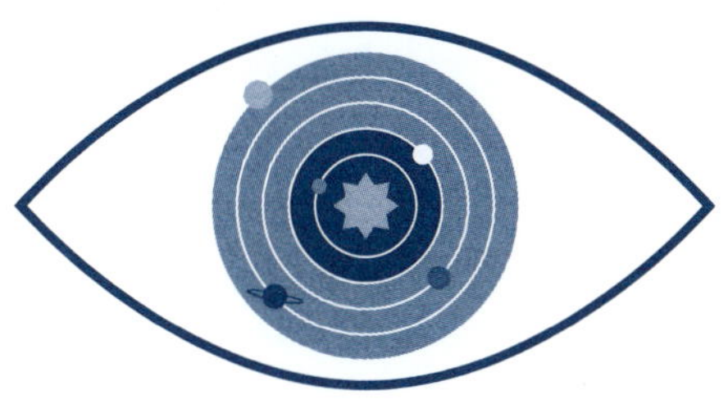

SHAWN ROBBINS • LEANNA GREENAWAY

STERLING ETHOS
New York

STERLING ETHOS and the distinctive Sterling Ethos logo are registered trademarks of Hachette Book Group, Inc.

© 2026 Leanna Greenaway and Shawn Robbins

All rights reserved. No part of this publication may be reproduced, stored in a retrieval system, or transmitted in any form or by any means (including electronic, mechanical, photocopying, recording, or otherwise) without prior written permission from the publisher.

The reader is advised that this book is not intended to be a substitute for an assessment by, and advice from, an appropriate legal, financial, or mental health professional or other qualified expert.

ISBN 978-1-4549-6302-8
ISBN 978-1-4549-6303-5 (e-book)

Library of Congress Control Number: 2025943159

Sterling Ethos books may be purchased in bulk for business, educational, or promotional use. For more information, please contact your local bookseller or the Hachette Book Group's Special Markets department at special.markets@hbgusa.com.

Printed in China

2 4 6 8 10 9 7 5 3 1

unionsquareandco.com

Cover design and illustration by Raphael Geroni
Interior images by Shutterstock.com: Murhena (stars), Salomi art (woman, backgrounds), Merfin (hands)
Interior design by Rich Hazelton

EVERY ONCE IN A WHILE, THE UNIVERSE SURPRISES US WITH A RARE GIFT

In Memory of Bill Gladstone, Our Beloved Agent

Bill, you touched our lives; you lit the flame that started our journey through the power of books and the written word. Although our time with you was limited, the memories are everlasting, and your profound impact on our hearts will be treasured.

Rest in peace, dear friend.

Leanna Greenaway and Shawn Robbins

Introduction

Since the dawn of time, people have been fascinated by fate, the Universe, and the meaning of life. These issues frequently spark intense philosophical, spiritual, and scientific debates, leading to interesting discussions in philosophy, religion, and science.

When we look up at the night sky or think about the Universe for any length of time, we are prompted to ask questions about mankind's existence and our place within this amazing creation.

Have you ever experienced a time in your life when you didn't know which way to turn? Have the challenges in your life been so complex that the only option is to reach out to the ether or a spiritual source and beg for a positive outcome? Even people who don't consider themselves religious may put their hands together and pray when things get tough.

In a world of uncertainty and chaos, many people turn to spiritual practices and beliefs for guidance and clarity. The concept of higher beings or spirit helpers providing us with insights and guidance from above has been around for centuries, and it is still very much alive in the hearts and minds of believers today. *Ask the Universe* explores this idea by giving readers an interactive experience of channeling a higher power. Look at it as a divination tool. Once you've mastered the art of channeling, you can unlock the secrets you've been looking for by asking the questions and turning the pages of this book to see the answers. Connecting to a higher power doesn't require being religious, but if you have a particular faith, whatever that may be, your main objective might be reaching out to your deity or spirit guide. We believe in spirit helpers, angels, and guides, but we also appreciate the power of the Universe and believe they are all somehow intertwined.

So many people visit psychics and mediums to find out details of their future or to make sense of their complicated lives. We know that clairvoyance is very real, but the gift of insight isn't just handed to a few lucky souls. All people have psychic abilities; some are open to them and welcome their strange intuitions, while others have the door closed and cannot focus on them. Even though our sixth senses vary in ability and strength, we all possess them. Much of the time, people will dismiss a strange or psychic moment as a coincidence and then, after the fact, may say something along the lines of, "I knew I shouldn't have left the house this morning," or "I was thinking about you earlier today, and you just called me!" All we need to do is master how to access and tap into our sixth sense. Humankind has always sought assistance from beyond, believing that spirit helpers possess a deeper understanding of the Universe and our place within it. Imagine having a direct line to the cosmos, a continual flow of guidance and wisdom from the divine source. Many believe that our spirit guides work closely with us while we journey through life and that, with practice, we can tap into this sacred source of inspiration to reveal their infinite wisdom. Although we may sometimes feel alone throughout our life's journey, we can take comfort in believing that a divine power supports us.

It's also interesting to note that thousands of people who have had near-death experiences (NDEs) have a similar understanding about the purpose of life. In these thousands of cases, people have talked about how every soul is a part of the Universe and how our earthly incarnations are only meant to aid in our souls' development. The *Next Level Soul* podcast, started by

Alex Ferrari, is an excellent and reliable source of information and is well worth a listen.

You've probably heard the sayings, "The universe/fate has brought us together" or "I think the universe is trying to tell me something." We believe that everything, good or evil, happens for a reason. Imagine life as a big school where we can reach the higher echelons by experiencing and dealing with challenging issues here on Earth. With every experience we encounter in life, good or bad, our soul will gain wisdom and knowledge. The reincarnation theory focuses on lesson learning; the more lives one has, the more the soul matures. This could help explain why certain people are so amiable, considerate, and kindhearted. Souls like this may have repeatedly reincarnated, going through various life lessons so they can now truly empathize with others. The same can be said for unpleasant or aggressive types; these might be young souls who are very new to the reincarnation process.

Whether or not you believe in reincarnation, you may question who is giving us the information we require when we do receive communications from an otherworldly source. Is it our gods, angels, or spirit guides, or are we speaking to the Universe directly?

Simply put, we don't know for sure, but we can confidently say that if you learn channeling techniques and reach out to the Universe or the spirit world for answers, it does work. A thought is a living thing; when we project our thoughts outward, they are picked up somewhere and given back to us in mysterious ways.

In a vast and incomprehensible Universe, it is comforting to think that there may be a higher power or force that acknowledges and respects the various ways humans express their spirituality. This idea challenges the notion of one true religion or faith and instead suggests that there is room for all beliefs in the grand scheme of the Universe.

How to Use This Book

This book explores how to connect with the higher, universal power—if you like, "the divine source." You'll learn how to quiet your mind, ask for guidance, and receive answers to your most pressing questions through meditations, prayers, rituals, and exercises.

The book you are holding now will become a divination tool, so it is essential that you take the time to properly respect and empower it. You can do that by following these steps:

Cleansing with Incense

To get rid of any bad energy, you need to perform a cleansing. This can be accomplished by burning sage or dragon's blood incense next to the book.

Sage: Sage is known for its purifying properties and is often used in smudging rituals to spiritually disinfect an area. It is also excellent at removing anything untoward or evil, so any negative energies will be eliminated.

Dragon's blood: In some cultures, this powerful resin incense is believed to bring good luck and protection. Like sage, it also wards off negative energies and purifies the space. It can be used in various spiritual practices, such as meditation or spellcraft. When used alongside sage, its power amplifies and eradicates any negative energies.

Cleansing with Crystals

You could use any number of crystals to sanctify your space and empower your book; if you have a vast knowledge of these precious stones, you can choose one or more of your favorites. For a more in-depth look at crystals and their magical influence, our book *The Crystal Witch* goes into great length about which stones are best utilized for various practices and offers more of a comprehensive look at crystals and their magical influence.

Selenite is known for its ability to clarify energy and is perfect for drawing out anything negative.

Clear quartz is a commanding crystal that increases the power of other crystals and stones.

Amethyst is a calming and soothing stone that can help promote a sense of inner peace and clarity.

Rose quartz works with the heart chakra and can help balance your emotions, allowing for a deeper connection with deities and the Universe.

To empower your book, move your chosen crystal in a slow circular motion over the cover and pages. If you prefer, you can place the crystal on top of the book and leave it there for a few hours. Close your eyes and imagine the stone absorbing any negative or sluggish energy from the book.

Meditation Space

For thousands of years, people from many cultures have been meditating with the same fundamental objective: to become aware of the present moment while tuning out the outside environment. It isn't always easy to master and may take practice, but by focusing on your intent while putting yourself in a relaxed state, it should be doable.

Step 1

Pick a quiet place where you won't be interrupted. This might be in a garden, a corner of your room, or anywhere you feel at ease.

Step 2

Play some calming music in the background to create a relaxing atmosphere. You can download lots of meditative tracks from the internet. Music is perfect for creating positive energy in your surroundings and assisting you in making a connection.

Step 3

Set a small table nearby and place a few candles on the surface. You could put some religious figurines or statues nearby to symbolize the presence of angels and deities or an image of the Universe. You can also place the same crystals you used for cleansing on the table. These will continue to amplify the energy.

Step 4

Find a comfortable place and position to sit or lie down; this might be in your favorite chair. You may prefer to rest on the bed if that is more relaxing or sit cross-legged on the floor.

Step 5

Shut your eyes gently to reduce outside distractions, or keep them slightly open and concentrate on the book in front of you.

Step 6

Pay attention to your breath. Breathe deeply through your nose for a few seconds, then gently release the breath through your mouth.

Step 7

While holding the book, think about the questions you want answers to. Continue with the visualization for about ten minutes.

Step 8

Hold the book and concentrate on your hands. They may feel tingly, or you might feel your pulse through your fingers. This is a sign that the book is ready to begin.

Other Items to Add to Your Table

In Step 3, you placed items of significance on your table to amplify the power of the meditation. By adding items like crystals, herbs, incense, and other components to your table, you can create the ideal atmosphere to encourage a closer relationship with the Universe. Put anything on the table that you consider to have symbolic power, since the sacred space you are creating is unique to you.

One item you could add to your altar is an incense burner. To create a peaceful atmosphere, use incense sticks or cones scented with lavender, sage, or chamomile. Sandalwood is also favorable, as it has a woody, earthy scent that is good for promoting grounding and stability. Frankincense is excellent for inspiring spiritual growth and connections to otherworldly beings, and finally, myrrh possesses a sweet, earthy scent that can help calm and soothe the mind.

Herbs

Lavender is known for its calming effects and can help soothe your mind and promote relaxation.

Chamomile is often used in teas and potpourri to promote relaxation and calmness. While sitting quietly with your book, perhaps sip some chamomile tea.

Angels and spirits love the smell of *mint* and are attracted to any variety.

Comforting Fabrics

Use soft, plush blankets or throw pillows to create a cozy and inviting space. Calming colors that promote relaxation are blue, green, or beige.

Preparing yourself and your environment for communication with the Universe can be a profound and enriching experience. Remember, you are part of the Universe, so establishing a connection shouldn't be too difficult.

Summoning the Universe and Spirit Helpers

Spirit guides are believed to be divine beings or entities that guide and support individuals on their earthly journey. While many people may seek guidance and assistance from their guides in times of need, it is essential to understand that there are times when they will not interfere in our lives because of the lessons we are meant to learn.

Spirit guides better understand the lessons we face here on Earth and function on a higher spiritual dimension. Interfering with these lessons would deprive us of the opportunity to grow, learn, and evolve as individuals. Sometimes we have to experience a situation in order to properly understand it, and although spirit guides can offer assistance and direction, it is our responsibility to make choices, grow, and learn from our experiences.

When performing divination, an invisible portal usually opens when someone establishes communication with the spirit world. It is crucial to allow only positive beings to pass through the doorway, so words of protection must be said before divination and communication with other worldly beings.

Light some white candles (for purification) and say this incantation: *I call upon the Universe to bathe me in a positive light. Allow only good to pass through the veil and shield me from anything dark or untoward.*

Hold the book in your hands and say this out loud:

I hereby Summon the Universe [or your deity].

I humbly invite you to be present and guide me as I open this book. Please bless all the pages with your light and love, illuminating the words and wisdom within. Help me connect with the messages and advice in these pages and guide me in applying them to my life in a way that brings me peace, clarity, and healing.

Next, while speaking aloud, tell the book what you wish to know. Make sure your words are clear and concise. For example, if you want to know the outcome of a situation, say, *I am unhappy in my employment. My bosses expect too much from me. I am stressed and tired. I am seeking a new job and working hard to find one. Is a new job around the corner for me? Will I change my employment soon?*

You may simply need some guidance. Perhaps you have a decision to make and are unsure of which direction to take. Give the Universe as much information as possible and say, for example, *I hope to move house in the coming months but am struggling to decide which property to choose. Please guide me in the right direction. Do I choose house A* [give the address] *or house B* [give the address]?

Receiving the Answers

Flip through the pages of the book repeatedly with your thumb for about sixty seconds, all the while asking the question out loud. When you feel ready, stop thumbing the pages, open the book, and point to whichever page is open. Your message will be in front of you, or it might be on the facing page—so look at both. You can ask the same question as many times as you like, and if the message doesn't relate to your question, simply try again. Sometimes it can take around five minutes of continually asking the same question before you get your answer. If none of the messages make sense, don't despair; it could be that you failed to make a connection and will need to try again another day. Not being in the right frame of mind, feeling under the weather, or simply being tired can be some of the reasons you might fail to establish that crucial link. As we have stated above, sometimes the Universe cannot interfere too much because it's your destiny to decide for yourself. Life is all about learning lessons and climbing the spiritual ladder. An otherworldly answer might influence a lesson you must learn.

Once you master the art of channeling and the connection is made, your answers should come through clearly and quickly.

You will also know when you have made a connection with the Universe because you will feel a sense of inner peace. Some people describe it as a floaty feeling, while others experience goose bumps. The answer can often be specific, so it may take your breath away for a few moments.

You could have a straightforward "yes" or "no" response. Don't feel despondent if you are in a position where you really desire something but the book steers you in a different direction.

When we look back on the past, we can often see why we weren't "allowed" to follow a particular path; if we did, we wouldn't have the life we are presently living or the people in it. This is frequently the case in romantic relationships. You may long for a specific individual's attention, but the book will present opposing viewpoints and dissuade you from pursuing them. The

Universe may have other ideas, and your fate is to end up with someone completely different. For example, if a certain relationship had occurred, you wouldn't meet your ideal partner and wouldn't start the family destined for you. Most things in our lives are preordained, and the Universe has this uncanny way of giving us exactly what we need. There are those who think we establish a soul contract before we come to this world, agreeing to share our lives with certain people and go through specific experiences; this may help to explain why we frequently find ourselves unintentionally led in one direction or another.

Record Your Messages

Often the book might foretell future events, and it would be a shame to forget them; with this in mind, it's always a good idea to record your findings. You can write down your questions before any channeling takes place and then note the responses below. You might prefer to use your phone to dictate the questions and answers.

Closing the Connection

Take a few deep breaths to acknowledge the communication and thank the Universe for its guidance.

If you're religious, you might like to say a prayer. Something like, *[Deity], I thank you for assisting me with your guidance. Please continue to protect and support me.*

When you have completed your breaths or the prayer, blow out the candles to symbolize the end of the channeling.

Clear your space by opening windows, lighting a smudging stick, or burning sage to cleanse residual energies.

Following these steps, you'll be well-equipped to connect with the Universe and receive guidance on your journey.

Answers

You've had
a hard time.
It would help
to have some
quiet time
to reflect
on recent issues.

Trust that you are protected more than you know.

When you feel at a low ebb, remember that you are loved by your spirit helpers.

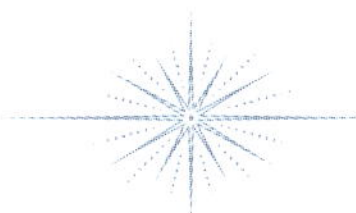

Candle flames light the way. Each night, burn a white candle to gain clarity.

The Universe has plans for you. Be patient and all will become clear in time.

Divine guidance leads to blessings. Things will improve soon.

Family is a source of strength, so confide in a loved one for the answers you seek.

Communication between you and someone else is stifled. Make more effort to be open and communicative.

A loved one in spirit is watching over you.

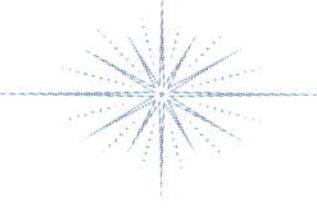

Times are
hard right now,
but have faith
as this phase
will soon end.

No, nothing is happening right now. The path ahead is blocked.

Look after your health and eat a balanced diet. Avoid temptation.

True friends understand you, but one may need your help soon, so make yourself available.

There is more than one family issue to deal with right now. Try to be patient and deal with them one at a time.

The answer is no.

Your intuition always leads you in the right direction.

You are holding the fort all on your own. Start delegating.

Raise your spiritual vibration. This is the reason you are living.

Yes, but things may take a little while to transpire.

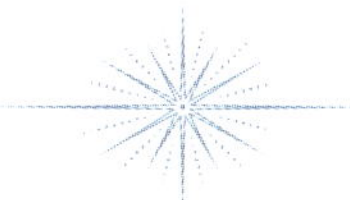

Yes, change is coming; remain strong and all will be well.

Angels whisper messages of hope. Concentrate on your third eye chakra to connect to your angel.

There are better paths to take. Perhaps rethink your options.

Embrace change with open arms, as a shift is about to take place in your life.

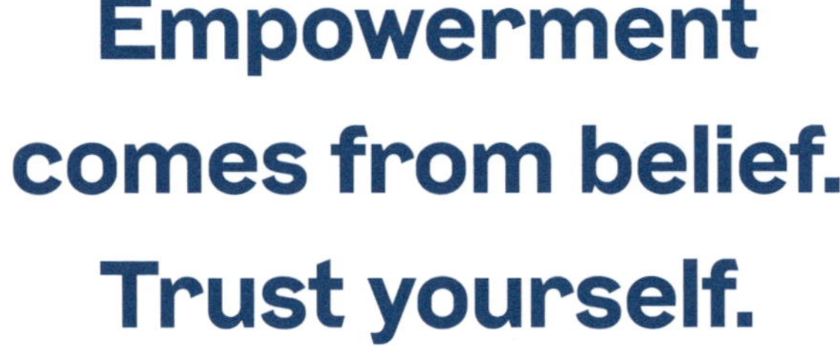

Empowerment comes from belief. Trust yourself.

Life is dull. Open yourself to new possibilities and opportunities that broaden your perspective.

Write down your wishes on paper and keep them in your mind's eye. You can manifest the things you want.

Romance will soon blossom, either within a marriage or established partnership, or in a brand-new relationship. Light a pink candle for love.

Show those around you how much you care. Make time for a partner or friend.

Just as
weather changes
constantly,
things may
be difficult for
a while, but the
storm will pass.

You are so tired; you need to take care of yourself.

Don’t sit and ponder; act now. Follow your heart.

You will need to make a decision soon, so think about it carefully. Don't rush.

You'll be faced with a problematic individual. Keep calm and maintain your composure. You're being spiritually tested.

If you are single, don't give away your heart too freely. Someone you meet is not worthy of you.

Personal growth is a journey. It's not always easy, but you are on the right path.

Not yet. Wait for the right time.

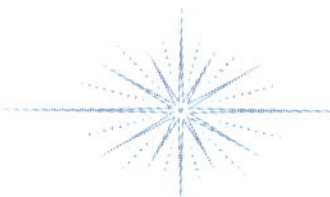

Listen to divine messages closely.

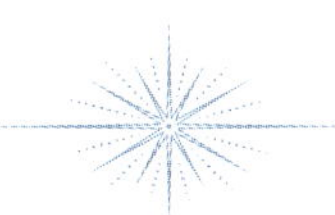

Believe in the Universe's plan. You will get everything you want but only when it's ready to happen.

New opportunities are coming. Grab them with both hands.

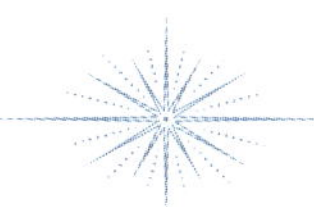

Work colleagues might be grumpy and ill-tempered. Maintain your composure.

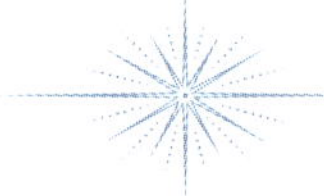

A fantastic new person will enter your life.

Form bonds with new people, explore a new interest, or enroll in a course.

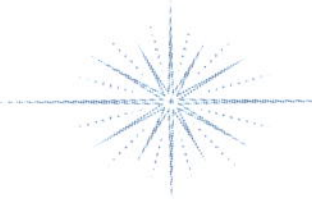

Yes, the way will be made clear.

Be patient. Things will happen in the coming months.

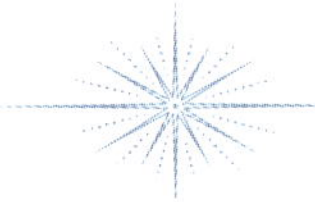

You need to step outside the box and look at things differently.

You may feel sad or weepy. Your guide is with you all the time. You are loved.

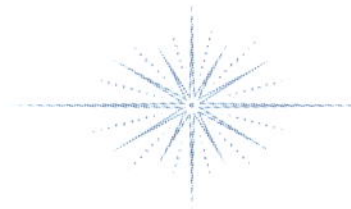

The situation you find yourself in is hard, but you chose to learn these lessons in life to elevate your subconscious. You are capable of passing the tests.

Friction in the family can be tiresome and quarrels may upset you. Time to put your foot down and take charge.

A family member, friend, or close acquaintance will need your advice. Make sure to offer your time.

A significant change you have wanted for a long time is coming.

You are so busy
all the time.
It helps to
take a break.

Get minor health niggles sorted by seeing a medical professional.

Work could be trying, and you may want to change direction. Do it now because everything is in place for your future.

You will feel much better about everything when the summer months come in.

You will have more than one romantic partner. Someone new will arise later. You will learn from every person who enters your life.

Try to be more creative and embrace a new activity. You have talents that have yet to come to fruition.

No, things will stay the same for a while.

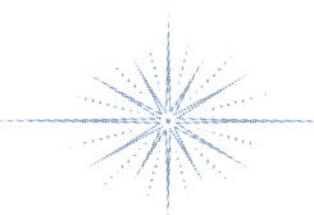

Don't pursue this avenue. Try another path.

You are psychic, but you need to open up to it more. To enhance your abilities, try joining a group that teaches spiritual development. Embracing and honing these skills can lead to more significant insights and experiences.

You must trust your intuition. Your spirit helpers will change your thinking and warn you of disruptive people.

You have tried and tried, and nothing seems to change. Try venturing down a different path now.

Your efforts have not gone unnoticed. The Universe is happy with your progress in this life.

Yes, get ready for positive changes.

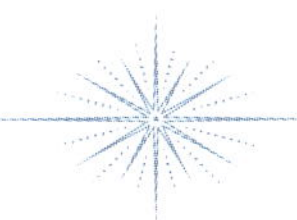

A man around you could be complex and hard to like. Stand up for yourself, and don't let him walk over you.

The answer is unclear.

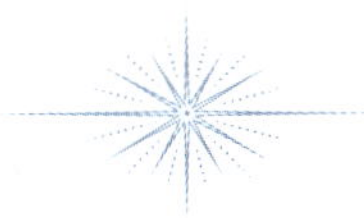

Are you really happy in your relationship? Try to connect again, and if that fails, consider your options.

Yes, a new beginning awaits you, but you must strive for it and not let it slip by.

The spirit guides have meaningful plans for you, leading to new opportunities and experiences. Embrace the journey ahead and trust the guidance you receive.

Yes, good news.

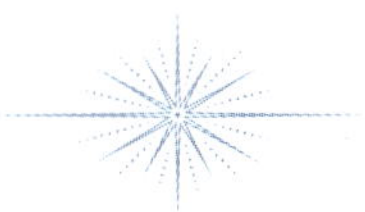

No, not yet, but have faith, things will get better in time.

Small changes can lead to important improvements in your life.

Spirit guides are like gentle whispers of wisdom and comfort in our journey through life. Your guide is unwavering and is watching over you all day.

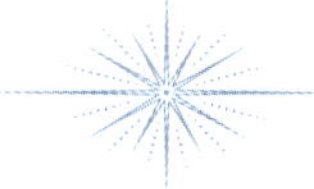

You may have to navigate relationship problems or be bickering with someone you once loved. Try to show empathy and understanding as they face their challenges.

You will start a new chapter in your career. It's an exciting opportunity to embark on a new journey filled with possibilities.

Life is looking up, and the journey to better days is truly something to celebrate.

A transition to a new property is on the horizon, offering fresh opportunities and experiences. This change will bring excitement and growth, leading to a positive chapter in your life.

Life will be pretty challenging, but better things are to come after the storm clears.

No, not at this time.

The answer is yes!

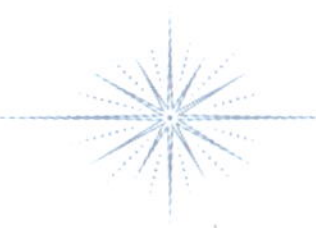

You must take some quiet time to contemplate and reflect on your recent challenges.

Someone is not what they seem; they have a dual nature. Be cautious with your trust.

A cherished person is facing challenges. Take the time to listen and understand their concerns, offering support and assistance to help them navigate their difficulties.

A spirit guide is with you and has been present since you were a child.

Exercise caution to avoid deception or scams. Be vigilant and responsible with your finances.

Yes,
things will
improve.

Try not to be in so much of a rush. Everything will arrive when it's meant to.

In the future, a friendship will end. For a short time you may find it difficult to trust others.

The answer is yes, but you have to wait.

Try not to settle for second best or allow someone else to make decisions for you. You deserve better.

You may be suffering from stress. Techniques such as deep breathing, meditation, or mindfulness can help.

Try to eradicate bad habits. Your health will suffer if you don't.

It's okay to say no. Protect your time and energy by setting boundaries.

Open up your psychic abilities by learning to meditate.

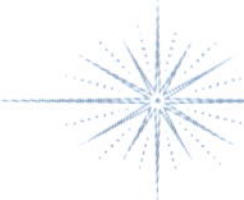

We can only get what we want sometimes. In this case, your life will take a different path.

Life often takes unexpected turns. It's essential to pause and appreciate what you already have.

Money may be scarce for some time. It's vital to cut back on expenses and plan more effectively.

Unexpected cash will come your way.

You might find yourself waiting for things to shift. Stay patient until June, and they will eventually unfold.

Unleash your creative side. All work and no play makes for a gray day.

Yes, the way will be made clear during the spring.

It's important to stay strong right now and make the right choices.

Within one year, you could be thinking about moving house.

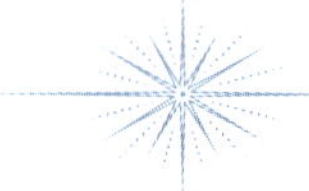

An ex can sometimes be challenging to deal with. It's essential to approach the situation with respect and kindness.

No. Obstacles surround you for a reason; you're on a learning curve.

Children will be a significant part of your life and bring immense joy, but set boundaries for them.

Embrace your creativity by writing a book or documenting your thoughts.

Try to focus on the spiritual aspect of your life. It invites a deeper connection with the Universe.

Perhaps.

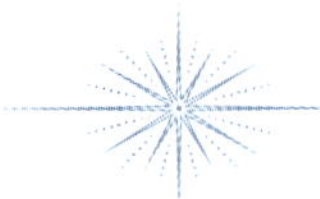

Life is about to change for the better; get ready for brighter days ahead.

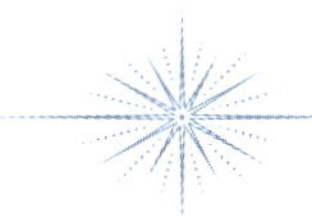

You will soon encounter challenges, so prepare yourself adequately and everything will work out fine.

Stop and think this through.

The answer is no, but you will understand why in due time.

You have lived many lives before; this is just another one where you have chosen to learn valuable lessons. Don't be surprised if you have déjà vu.

Navigating family relations can sometimes be taxing, but patience is key to maintaining harmony.

There is a breakdown in communication with someone.

The answer is yes; change is coming soon.

A past love will not let go.

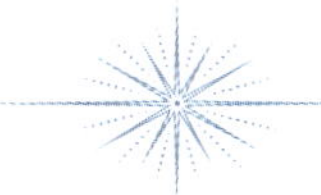

It may be time for a change if you are bored with your current job.

Believe in yourself; you can achieve anything you set your mind to.

An obnoxious person may bring you down and leave you feeling dejected. Still, it's essential to rise above it and not let them affect you.

Not everything works out how we would like, but we must maximize what we have.

Yes,
things are about
to start moving.

The Universe has a plan for you; everything is meant to be. Trust in the guidance you receive, and the reasons will become more apparent in due time.

No.

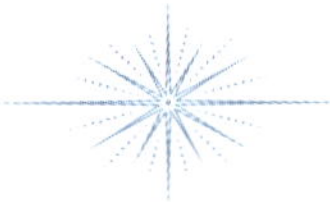

Concentrate on your question and ask again for a more precise answer.

Yes, rest assured that your wishes will be fulfilled.

Tomorrow is another day. You may not feel you are walking the right path, but you are exactly where you are meant to be.

The answer is deep within you. Search your heart to find the truth.

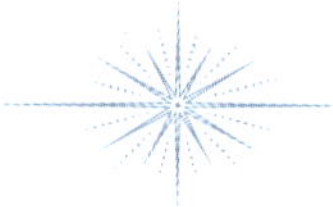

Yes.

Your luck is about to change for the better.

Do not fret
about money;
be cautious with
your spending
and everything
will be fine.

The Universe does not know the answer to your question.

Look out for a sign from the spirit world. They want you to know they are beside you always.

You have experienced a difficult time in your life. Keep positive, as this challenging period will soon end.

You could be worried about someone close. Meditate and you will be given the answers you need.

You know deep down this is not right for you.

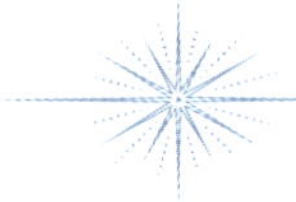

You currently have a strong guide in the spirit world who watches over you and ensures your protection and well-being.

An excellent job opportunity will come your way, and the future appears promising.

Arguments and upsets can leave you feeling broken, but with communication and understanding, healing is possible.

You know the answer already. Trust your instincts.

You are at a crossroads, unsure of which path to take and faced with decisions that must be made. Remember, you have the freedom to choose.

You may not be sleeping well or you may be waking up multiple times a night. Try lavender oil.

A lump sum of money will be arriving soon; make sure to spend it wisely.

The emotional burden you bear is dragging you down. Choose what is right for you and prioritize your well-being.

Muster some courage and forge ahead.

Have you been thinking about a loved one who has passed? They still walk beside you.

Wishes will be granted, and celebrations will be on the horizon.

You will finally get what you have been wanting.

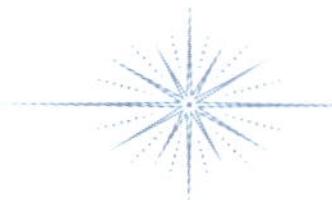

Something treasured is lost. You will find it eventually.

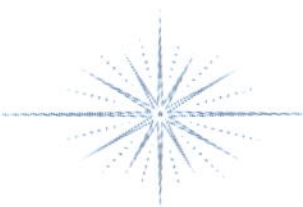

You possess the ultimate spiritual shield, protecting you from all negativity and harm.

Your life is in a never-ending cycle; it's time to break free and forge a new path.

An ordinarily happy relationship will face challenges. Work through the issues and compromise.

Take the leap and explore a new course or hobby; you have the potential to thrive and excel.

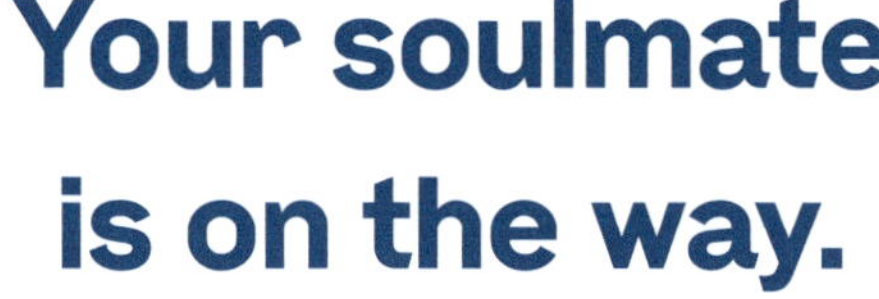

Your soulmate
is on the way.

Someone is jealous of you. Try to be kind to them.

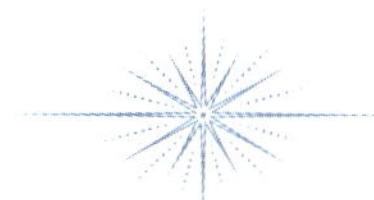

You may have had some bad news. Allow yourself time to reflect.

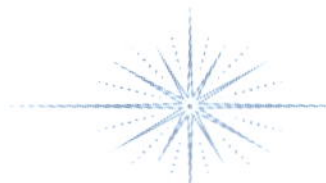

Someone is thinking about you.

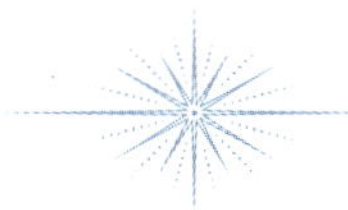

Leave the past behind you and focus on creating a brighter future. Dwelling on what has happened will not change anything.

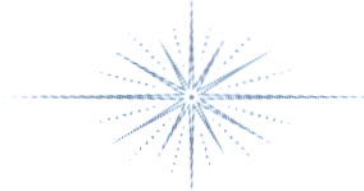

Maybe.

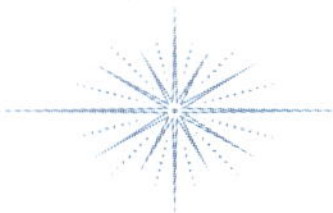

Trust your instincts regarding people; there's always a bad apple in the barrel.

No, don't do anything rash; the perfect time is ahead.

A work colleague will upset you. Take no heed of it.

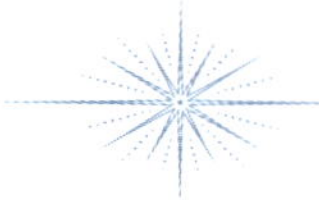

You will feel hopeless, but stick with it because things will improve quickly.

You chose to reincarnate with difficult people for a reason. Do the best you can.

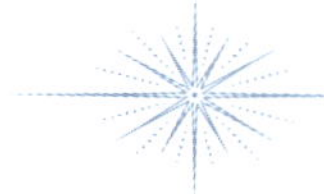

You will feel under the weather, so staying home and resting is best.

You are always putting others first. For a change, do something for yourself.

The thought of changing address is being considered, possibly indicating a move out of the area.

No, it's not the right time.

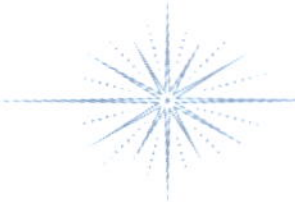

Traveling to exotic lands is an excellent way to spend a vacation.

It’s unlikely.

Autumn is a better time for you. Look forward to it.

Do not allow yourself to be swayed into behaving in a way that goes against your true character; the consequences will not be good.

It is time to carefully consider the future of your relationships and make some critical decisions.

Yes, eventually. There is a waiting time.

No, this will steer you away from your intended path.

Don't let others drag you down with their problems; choose to detach and not become too invested.

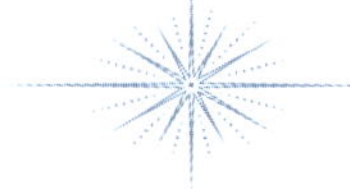

Not now
or ever.

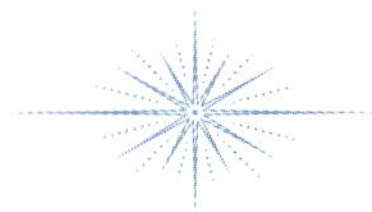

Don’t put up with things. Make a change.

When faced with a blocked road, it is a sign that you are not meant to continue down that path.

Someone does not deserve your love. You know who this is.

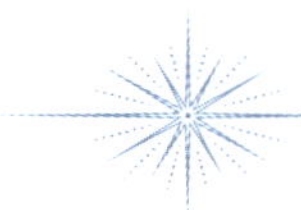

No,
walk away.

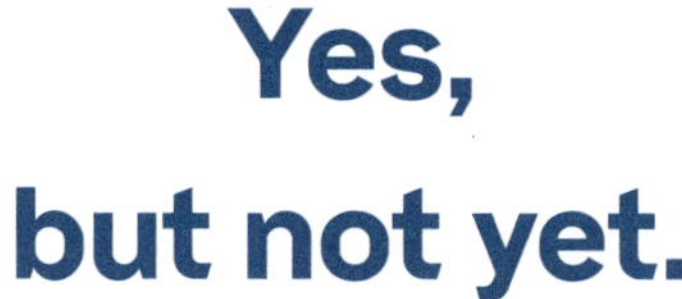
Yes,
but not yet.

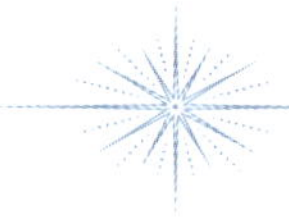

Your guardian angel is protecting you.

Focus on something else.

The load you are carrying is heavy. Share your troubles with others.

Keep good hygiene in mind, and avoid colds and bugs.

A small boy is either in your life or will make an appearance.

A dark-haired man will enter your life and make a difference.

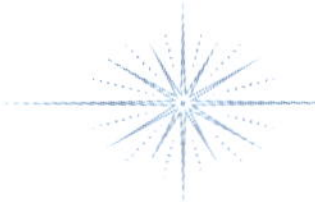

It's the end of an era. As one door closes, another will open.

Travel by air.

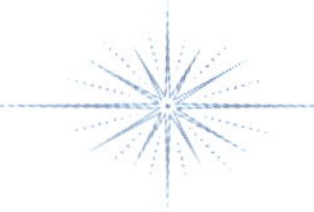

A reunion is highly recommended. Meet up with people from the past.

You are worried and are not sure which way to turn. Have faith; all will be well.

The Universe is still trying to figure out the answer.

Try not to dwell on things you can't change. If you can't accept the situation, step away from it.

Yes, the disruption will soon be over.

Spend wisely because unexpected bills will drop on the mat.

Essential emails and letters are on their way.

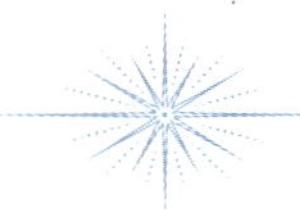

Yes, things will improve.

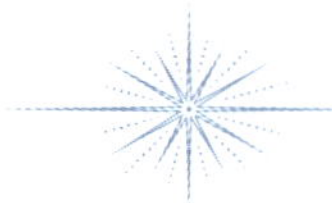

Love and passion will ignite in your life, filling every corner with warmth and intensity.

Life is too short
to be serious
all the time,
so relax, kick
back, and enjoy
some leisure time.

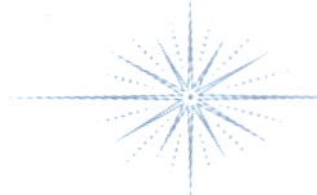

It's time to let go of the past and move forward toward a brighter future.

Don’t allow the bad moods of others to bring you down. Cut ties with toxic individuals and prioritize your own well-being.

You have a team of guides leading you through life's lessons, and through your choices you are evolving into a better soul.

Overeating or consuming too much alcohol can lead to poor decision-making. It is essential to combat these addictions and cleanse your soul.

You spend your life making others' lives better. Remember to take some time for yourself.

No one has the right to mistreat you. Stand firm, and don't be pushed around.

Everything will work out well in the end.

Friends are important. Make time for them.

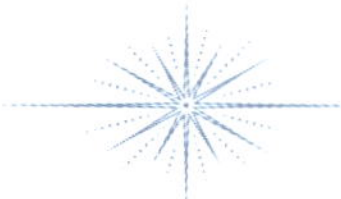

Victory is yours after a time of struggle.

A brand-new job is coming.

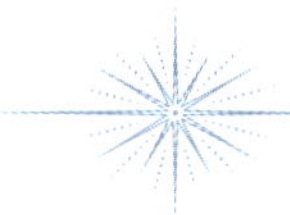

A legal issue could take place this year.

Trust your instincts if you suspect someone is being disloyal.

You will offer a shoulder for someone to cry on. Make time to help another through a difficult time.

Even though they
are no longer
physically present,
your loved one
in spirit is always
with you.

Sometimes we must backtrack to get on the right path.

The Universe doesn't know the answer to this question. Be more specific.

Be on your guard at work; someone isn't as trustworthy as they seem.

Joy and happiness
are forecast
for the future.
Today's problems
will disappear
soon.

You have a new path to take in life. Are you brave enough to venture into unknown territory?

After a problematic relationship, a new and improved one will follow.

A person you hold in high regard does not reciprocate those feelings. Cut your ties.

Your future will reveal the truth. You are meant to know later.

A long-lost friend has resurfaced, and a reunion is in the cards.

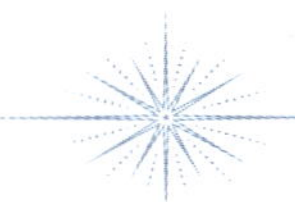

You may not get what you want right now, but amazing things are forecast for the future.

You are finding life a struggle at the moment. This difficult time is just a phase, and things will improve.

There are better ways forward.

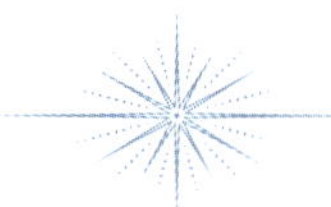

Someone is concealing the truth.

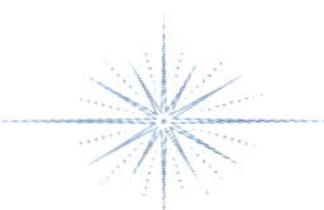

No,
it's the
wrong time.

The person you desire is not available.

Your soulmate is in the spirit world. For your spiritual growth and learning, you must experience other relationships.

The Universe says yes.

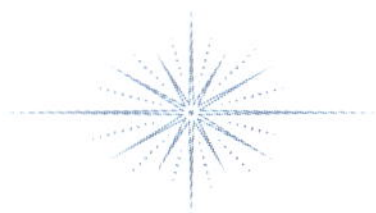

No, this is the wrong choice to make.

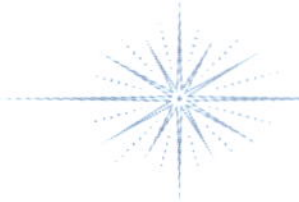

Your ideas are planted in your mind for a reason. Act on them.

Someone always has their hand out for money. Say no!

Exciting wonders are on the horizon; prepare for life to take a turn for the better!

With all the family gatherings and friends wanting to catch up, you'll be kept on your toes! Just remember not to overwhelm yourself by taking on too much!

If your confidence were to be compromised, remember that you are worth more than you know. Stay strong and believe in yourself.

The Universe is poised for you to embark on a new journey.

Manifest your desires. Focus on what you want and believe it will happen. That's how magic works.

A year from now, you will look back on today and have a completely different mindset.

Try not to overthink things; the answer is straightforward.

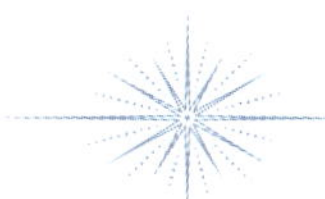

It is not believed to be so.

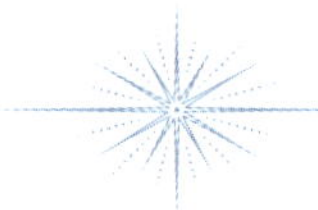

Yes, it is believed so.

You keep relearning old lessons. Walk away and find an alternative path.

Raise your standards and find people on the same wavelength as yourself.

You deserve to be loved and cherished. Make sure you have the right people in your life.

This life will throw many challenges, but you are never given any lesson you can't cope with.

When you sleep, you visit the celestial realms. Pay attention to messages you receive there. Keep a dream journal and record the details to help decipher your dreams.

Maybe.

Surround yourself with soothing crystals. You are sensitive to their power.

No, you need to focus on other things right now.

Take time to travel or escape the daily grind for a while. It will be good for your soul.

Don't worry about things that have yet to happen. It is wasted energy, and life will invariably take a different turn.

Respect yourself more. Don't let others order you around. This is your life, and you are in control of it.

Times are tough, but remember, this is just a temporary situation that will pass soon.

Someone might need your support soon, so be ready to lend a hand.

Focus on your third eye chakra to tune into your angel's presence.

Be open to new experiences and ideas to spark your mind and keep things interesting.

If you are single, new romance is on the horizon. If you are in a relationship, happy times are ahead.

Embrace change with a positive attitude. It might be challenging, but these times won't last forever.

Don’t just think about it; take action right away.

Don’t be tempted by another’s affections.

A decision is coming up, so choose wisely.

You will be dealing with a demanding person. Just stay calm and keep your cool.

You've got more magic inside you than you realize. Hone your skills.

Trust that the Universe has a plan for you, and that divine guidance will lead you.

It's time to consider a career shift; look for new job options.

Romance is on the horizon, so get ready to connect with someone unique.

Speak up, and don't just watch from the sidelines.

Start a new hobby, sign up for a class, or learn a new skill. You might shock yourself at how well you do.

The right path will become evident.

Yes, and everything will turn out fine.

You might feel down or emotional, but remember, your guide is always by your side. These challenging experiences you're facing are meant to help you grow on a deeper level.

A significant change you've been hoping for is finally on the way.

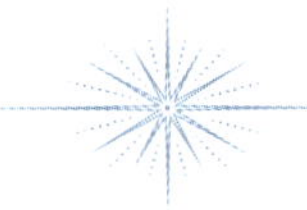

Throughout your life, you'll find yourself in multiple romantic relationships, but there's someone special waiting for you down the line.

You have psychic abilities that could flourish if you allow yourself to explore them more. Consider joining a group to help develop those skills.

Trust your gut feelings; your spiritual guides are there to shift your perspective and alert you to negative influences.

If you feel stuck despite your efforts, take a different approach and see where it leads.

Your hard work hasn't gone unnoticed; the Universe is pleased with how far you've come in this life.

There might be a woman around you who's tough to deal with, so stand your ground and don't let her push you around.

There's more to someone than meets the eye; they might have a hidden side. Be careful about who you trust.

You will do so well at work, you'll be given a pat on the back.

Things will get better, so hang in there. Good things are coming your way in the future.

Take action toward your goals to steer your life in your desired direction.

When you're feeling worn out, permit yourself to take a break without feeling bad about it.

The answer is yes, but be patient. The path ahead will become more apparent.

Start a journal to record your thoughts, emotions, and growth; it can help you better understand your life.

Work is demanding with very little reward. Consider a different path.

Not at this time.

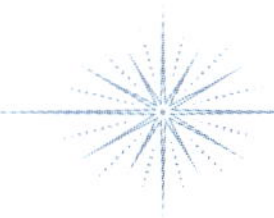

You may be saying goodbye to a friend. Someone is set to embark on a new path.

Money may be tight for a while. Set some aside for a rainy day if you can.

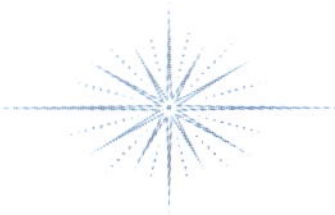

Embrace your dreams and try to make them come true. The Universe favors you right now.

Something extraordinary will happen this year. Embrace change.

Your life has been challenging, but you chose to experience these life lessons. They will shape you into the person you are meant to be.

New friendships flourish in the next few months. Someone lovely will enter your life.

Dedicate more time and energy to nature and animals. For clarity, go walking in the woods or visit a beach. Go outdoors and smell the flowers. Time with nature is essential.

You might feel dejected at work or have more to give. Consider looking for new employment.

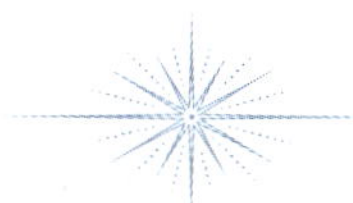

Don't be afraid to tell someone close to you exactly how you feel. You can only advance when everything is out in the open.

Keep small items safe. You might lose something small, like jewelry or keys.

Let go of feelings of failure. You have not failed; you are learning valuable lessons. You cannot change what has happened, but you can move forward positively.

The answer to your question is not clear. Please ask another one.

Forgive someone who has hurt you. They are not as spiritually evolved as you are.

You can't always get exactly what you want, but something just as lovely is coming.

Someone who has passed away is still very much in your life. They keep an eye on you all the time.

Not this time; maybe later.

You need to cheer yourself up. Do something fun and exciting.

You have reincarnated many times. This life is just one of many, and more will come when this life is over.

Organize your life better. Walk away from difficult people and make new friends who resonate with your vibration.

Let go of
your worries.
None of them will
come to pass.

Someone is constantly thinking about you.

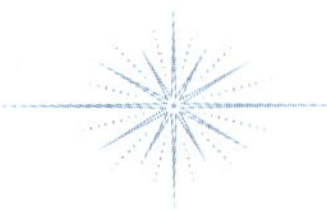

Yes, it would seem so!

About the Authors

Shawn Robbins is the author or coauthor of numerous books, including six in the Modern-Day Witch series: *The Holistic Witch*, *Psychic Spellcraft*, *The Witch's Way*, *The Crystal Witch*, *The Good Witch*, the forthcoming *Numbers Witch*, and *Wiccapedia*, a bestseller that is now used as a reference guide in many online Wicca schools. She has taught classes about herbs, health, and healing at the New York School of Occult Arts and lectures extensively throughout the country on these subjects. She lives in New York State.

Leanna Greenaway is a popular British clairvoyant who has appeared on TV and radio and was a columnist for the UK's *Fate & Fortune* magazine. She is the author or coauthor of many books, including *The Holistic Witch*, *Psychic Spellcraft*, *The Witch's Way*, *The Crystal Witch*, *Wiccapedia*, *Simply Tarot*, *Witchcraft: An Introduction*, and the forthcoming *Numbers Witch*. You can follow her on her YouTube channel. She lives in South West England.